DIOSITO Y CAFECITO

PRAYERS PARA LLEVAR

EVELYNE PÉREZ

Diosito y cafecito: Prayers para llevar
Published by Evelyne Pérez
Copyright © 2025 by Evelyne Pérez

Written by Evelyne Pérez
ISBN: 979-8-9905164-9-6

Para mi mamá, Sandra, mis hermanas, Brenda y Claudia, y todas las mujeres fuertes en mi vida:
Ustedes son como la luna llena, iluminando el desierto con la luz de su fe.

Contents:

Introduction:	1
For the Days You Feel Overwhelmed:	2-3
For When You're Stuck in Traffic:	4-5
For Family Drama:	6-7
For the Blessing of a New Day:	8-9
For the Gift of Friendship:	10-11
For Times of Uncertainty:	12-13
For Patience:	14-15
For a Broken Heart:	16-17
For Guidance in Decisions:	18-19
For Gratitude:	20-21
For Finding "The One":	22-23
For a Struggling Relationship:	24-25
For Healing:	26-27
For Strength During Sickness:	28-29
For a Job Opportunity:	30-31
For Financial Blessings:	32-33
For Birthdays:	34-35
For the New Year:	36-37
For Family:	38-39
For Nature's Beauty:	40-41
For Facing Challenges:	42-43

For New Beginnings: 44-45

For Safe Travels: 46-47

For a Peaceful Home: 48-49

For Overthinking: 50-51

For Understanding Others: 52-53

For Perseverance: 54-55

For Courage: 56-57

For Before a Meal: 58-59

For Those in Need: 60-61

For Stronger Faith: 62-63

For Spiritual Growth: 64-65

For Blessing Your Business: 66-67

For Strength: 68-69

For Hope: 70-71

For Anxiety: 72-73

For Grief: 74-75

For Unity: 76-77

For the Oppressed: 78-79

For Self-Love: 80-81

For Forgiveness: 82-83

For Inner Peace: 84-85

For Wisdom: 86-87

For Trust: 88-89

For Neighbors: 90-91

For Those Who Feel Alone: 92-93

For a Restful Night: 94-95

For Peace in the World: 96-97

For the Environment: 98-99

For Overcoming Fear: 100-101

For Our Children: 102-103

For Moving to a New Place: 104-105

For Starting a New Job: 106-107

For Students Taking Exams: 108-109

For Parents: 110-111

For Patience with Technology: 112-113

For Feeling Lost: 114-115

For Protection Against Enemies: 116-117

Against Tarnishing of Name: 118-119

For Motivation: 120-121

For Discipline to Keep Answered Prayers: 122-123

For Work: 124-125

For Children with Disabilities: 126-127

Note from the Author: 128-129

Books by the Author: 130-131

Introduction:

Welcome to *Diosito y Cafecito,*
a little book made with love, faith,
and a whole lot of *cafecito.*

Think of this *libro de oraciones*
like the sweater your *mamá*
made you keep handy in 97° weather—
por si acaso.

Inside, you'll find prayers
for everyday struggles,
created to bring a little peace
and remind you that *Diosito*
is always with you—
even in traffic, family drama,
or when someone takes
the last *pan dulce.*

So grab your *cafecito*, take a pause,
and let's connect with
nuestro Diosito lindo.

"I can do all things through
Christ which strengtheneth me."

(Philippians 4:13, KJV)

Prayer for the Days You Feel Overwhelmed:

Diosito,

Today my to-do list is longer than my
abuela's stories.
Give me strength, *paciencia*, and a little bit
of your divine *energía* to tackle each task.
Help me remember that I don't have to do
it all at once.
That it's okay to pause, breathe,
and take it one step at a time…
contigo a mi lado.

¡Amén!

"Be still, and know that I am God: I will be exalted among the heathen, I will be exalted in the earth."

(Psalm 46:10, KJV)

Prayer for When You're Stuck in *Traffic:*

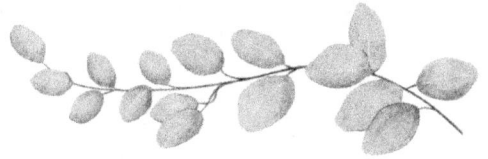

Diosito,

Blessed are those who arrive on time,
pero ahorita I'm stuck in this
never-ending traffic.
Grant me *paciencia* and remind
me that there's a bigger plan.
Help me use this time to
pause, reflect, and send good vibes
to all the other souls in their *carros.*
Contigo, even this moment has purpose.

¡Amén!

"Forbearing one another, and forgiving one another, if any man have a quarrel against any: even as Christ forgave you, so also do ye."

(Colossians 3:13, KJV)

Prayer for

Family Drama:

Diosito,

You know how much I love my *familia*…
pero sometimes they really
test my *paciencia*.
Give me the wisdom to navigate
our *pláticas* with love and understanding.
And remind me that
"¿te calmas o te calmo?"
has never actually solved anything…
and neither has threatening
to throw the *chancla*.
Help us find common ground
and remind me
that *la familia* is everything.

¡Amén!

"It is of the Lord's mercies that we are not consumed, because his compassions fail not. They are new every morning: great is thy faithfulness."

(Lamentations 3:22-23, KJV)

Prayer for the Blessings of a
New Day:

Diosito,

Thank you for this new day, full of
possibilities and new beginnings.
Hoy, let me not spill the *cafecito*
or lose my keys (*otra vez*).
Help me find joy in the little *cositas* and
share good vibes with everyone I meet.
May my smile be bright like the sun
and my *paciencia* as long as a *novela*.
May I spread positivity and be a light to
others today.

¡Amén!

"A friend loveth at all times, and a brother is born for adversity."

(Proverbs 17:17, KJV)

Prayer for the Gift of
Friendship:

Diosito,

Gracias for the *comadres*
who feel more like *familia*
than some of my *primos.*
Bless their *corazones.*
Thank you for the kind of friendship
that survives busy schedules,
unanswered texts,
and life getting in the way.
May our bond stay strong—
stronger than my *tía's cafecito*
and our group chat *chisme.*
Help us *seguir echándonos porras,*
praying for one another,
and making sure nobody suffers alone.
And please bless the friend
who says, *"Amiga…* your guardian
angel is tired."

¡Amén!

"For I know the thoughts that I think toward you, saith the Lord, thoughts of peace, and not of evil, to give you an expected end."

(Jeremiah 29:11, KJV)

Prayer for the Times of

Uncertainty:

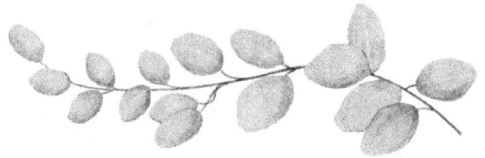

Diosito,

When I don't know what the future holds,
help me trust in your plan.
Give me the courage to step forward,
knowing you are guiding my path.
Fill me with *esperanza*
and remind me that everything
will be okay.

¡Amén!

"But let patience have her perfect
work, that ye may be perfect and
entire, wanting nothing."

(Santiago 1:4, KJV)

Prayer for

Patience:

Diosito,

Grant me patience—
when the line at the *tienda* is long,
when the internet is slow, *y cuando mi
novio/novia se tarda demasiado.*
Help me remember
that good things come to those who wait,
and that everything happens
in your perfect time.

¡Amén!

"He healeth the broken in heart,
and bindeth up their wounds."

(Psalm 147:3, KJV)

Prayer for a
Broken Heart:

Diosito,

My heart's been broken into
little pieces, like a *mazapán.*
Heal my wounds, mend my *espíritu,*
and help me see the love
that still surrounds me.
Remind me that I am strong,
that I am worthy,
and that I am capable of loving again.

¡Amén!

"I will instruct thee and teach thee in the way which thou shalt go: I will guide thee with mine eye."

(Psalm 32:8, KJV)

Prayer for Guidance in
Decisions:

Diosito,

I'm at a *"¿y ahora qué?"* moment
and I need your wisdom.
Light my path, open my *corazón*,
and help me choose the direction that
aligns with your will.
Give me the courage to follow your voice—
even when it's *difícil.*

¡Amén!

"In every thing give thanks: for this is the will of God in Christ Jesus concerning you."

(1 Thessalonians 5:18, KJV)

Prayer for
Gratitude:

Diosito,

Thank you for all the *bendiciones* in my life
—*las grandes y las pequeñas.*
For *cafecito* in my favorite *taza,*
pan dulce on slow mornings,
and time spent with the people I love.
But also for the moments
I once only dreamed about—
the doors you've opened,
the places you've taken me,
and the reminders that I belong there too.
Help me never lose gratitude
for the simple things
or the beautiful surprises along the way.
Fill my *corazón* with *humildad,*
apreciación y paz—
today, tomorrow, *y siempre.*

¡Amén!

"Whoso findeth a wife findeth a good thing, and obtaineth favour of the Lord."

(Proverbs 18:22, KJV)

Prayer for Finding
"The One":

Diosito,

If it's in your plan for me,
send that special someone my way.
Someone who understands my chaos,
loves my flaws,
and shares my *sueños.*
Someone who can handle me
on the days I can't get to my *cafecito…*
because without my morning coffee,
hasta yo me caigo mal.
Help me recognize them
and open my *corazón*
to the beautiful *aventura* of love.

¡Amén!

"Charity suffereth long, and is kind; charity envieth not; charity vaunteth not itself, is not puffed up,"

(1 Corinthians 13:4, KJV)

Prayer for a Struggling
Relationship:

Diosito,

We're hitting a rough patch,
and things feel more
like a *lucha libre* match.
Sometimes our *orgullo*
feels bigger than our love.
Help us remove the *máscaras*
and soften our hearts.
Teach us to communicate with kindness,
understand each other's *corazones,*
and remember why we fell in love.
Guide us toward healing
and renewed *cariño.*

¡Amén!

"Heal me, O Lord, and I shall be healed; save me, and I shall be saved: for thou art my praise."

(Jeremiah 17:14, KJV)

Prayer for
Healing:

Diosita,

Please heal the parts of me
that nobody sees.
The stress, the sadness,
the disappointments,
and the heaviness I carry quietly.
Wrap me in your *paz*
and remind me
that healing takes time.
Poquito a poquito,
help me feel like myself again.

¡Amén!

"A merry heart doeth good like a
medicine: but a broken spirit
drieth the bones."

(Proverbs 17:22, KJV)

Prayer for Strength

During Sickness:

Diosito,

Being sick is a major *bajón.*
Give me strength to get through this,
paciencia with my body,
and faith that I will recover.
Wrap me in a little
"sana sana colita de rana,"
reminding me I'll be okay.
I trust in your healing power
and know you are with me always.

¡Amén!

"But my God shall supply all
your need according to his riches
in glory by Christ Jesus."

(Philippians 4:19, KJV)

Prayer for a
Job Opportunity:

Diosito,

Ábreme las puertas in my career path,
por favor.
Guide me toward the *oportunidades*
that are meant for me.
Give me confidence in my abilities
and help me shine like *una estrella*
in my interviews.
I trust in your plan for my success—
échame la mano
to show them what I'm made of.

¡Amén!

"Bring ye all the tithes into the storehouse, that there may be meat in mine house, and prove me now herewith, saith the Lord of hosts, if I will not open you the windows of heaven, and pour you out a blessing, that there shall not be room enough to receive it."

(Malachi 3:10, KJV)

Prayer for
Financial Blessings:

Diosito,

Bendice mis finanzas,
especially when my cart says one thing
and my bank account says another.
Provide me with *lana para salir adelante,*
guide me to make smart decisions,
and remind me
que hay frijoles en la casa.
Help me use my *recursos*
to bless others—
especialmente a mi familia.

¡Amén!

"The Lord bless thee, and keep thee: The Lord make his face shine upon thee, and be gracious unto thee: The Lord lift up his countenance upon thee, and give thee peace."

(Numbers 6:24-26, KJV)

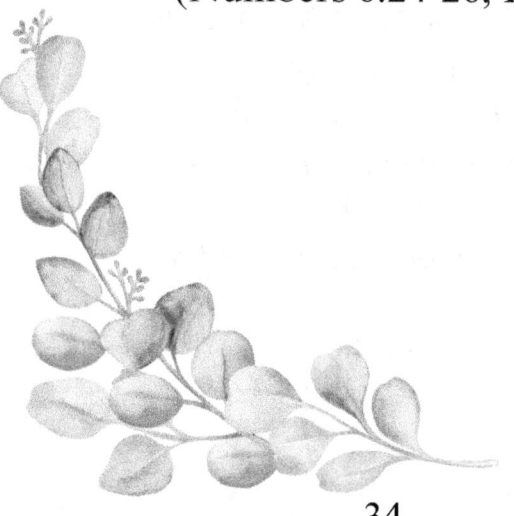

Prayer for
Birthdays:

Diosito,

Thank you for another year of life,
lessons, and *bendiciones*.
Help me celebrate with *alegría,*
appreciate the *gente en mi vida,*
and look forward to the *adventuras* ahead.
¡Que este día esté lleno de pastel y amor...
y que nadie me pregunte mi edad!

¡Amén!

"I press toward the mark for the prize of the high calling of God in Christ Jesus."

(Philippians 3:14, KJV)

Prayer for the
New Year:

Diosito,

As we start this *año nuevo,*
llénanos with hope, *inspiración,*
and the courage to pursue our dreams.
Bless our *planes,* guide our *pasos,*
and help us make a positive impact in the
world.
¡Que este año sea mejor que el pasado!

¡Amén!

"For this cause I bow my knees
unto the Father of our Lord
Jesus Christ, Of whom the whole
family in heaven and earth is
named,"

(Ephesians 3:14-15, KJV)

Prayer for
Family:

Diosito,

Bendice mi familia—
los que están cerca y lejos,
the ones I see every day
and the ones I miss deeply.
Keep them safe, healthy,
and *llenos de alegría.*
Help us support each other,
querernos un montón,
and remember that family
is one of life's greatest *bendiciones.*
Let our home always be filled
with laughter, *cafecito,* good food,
and leftovers packed in
empty butter containers.
Give us the kind of love
that feels like home
no matter where we are.

¡Amén!

"The heavens declare the glory of God; and the firmament sheweth his handywork."

(Psalm 19:1, KJV)

Prayer for
Nature's Beauty:

Diosito,

Thank you for the vibrant colors of the
flowers,
for *la arena morenita—*
un reflejo de nuestra piel,
for the soothing sounds of the rain
and the amazing smell of
tierra mojada after it falls—like home.
Help me notice the *belleza* in your
creation—to slow down, breath deeply,
and enjoy the world around me.
Let me find peace in nature
and share that joy with others.

¡Amén!

"God is our refuge and strength,
a very present help in trouble."

(Psalm 46:1, KJV)

Prayer for Facing
Challenges:

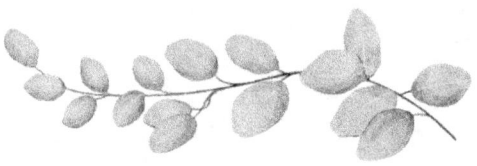

Diosito,

When the world feels *pesado* on my
shoulders,
dame la fuerza to rise above.
Give me courage to face my fears
and the wisdom
to learn from my struggles.
Help me remember that I am *fuerte—*
una guerrera,
like my *madre,*
my *abuelita,*
mis hermanas y mis tías.

¡Amén!

"And he that sat upon the throne said, Behold, I make all things new. And he said unto me, Write: for these words are true and faithful."

(Revelation 21:5, KJV)

Prayer for
New Beginnings:

Diosito,

As I step into this new chapter,
guide me with *tu luz*.
Help me embrace change
and trust in your plan, *aunque no lo
entienda todavía.*
Let me approach each day
with hope and excitement,
knowing you are with me
every step of the way.

¡Amén!

"The Lord shall preserve thee
from all evil: he shall preserve thy
soul."

(Psalm 121:7, KJV)

Prayer for
Safe Travels:

Diosito,

As I begin this journey,
please keep me safe from harm.
Watch over me *en el camino,*
en el cielo,
and in unfamiliar places.
Surround me with your protection
and bring me back home safely.

¡Amén!

"Through wisdom is an house builded; and by understanding it is established: And by knowledge shall the chambers be filled with all precious and pleasant riches."

(Proverbs 24:3-4, KJV)

Prayer for a
Peaceful Home:

Diosito,

Bless my *casa* with peace
and *tranquilidad.*
May these walls be filled with laughter,
our hearts with love,
and our spirits with harmony.
Protect us from negativity
and fill our home
with your divine presence.
And may everyone who walks in
feel your *paz* here.

¡Amén!

"Casting all your care upon him; for he careth for you."

(1 Peter 5:7, KJV)

Prayer for

Overthinking:

Diosito,

Please calm this mind of mine.
You know how
my thoughts spread faster
than my *tía* spreads *chisme*.
I replay conversations,
stress about things that haven't happened,
and start creating scenarios
that aren't even real.
Help me pause, breathe,
and stop feeding every worried thought.
Remind me that not everything
needs to be figured out tonight.
Fill my *corazón* with peace,
quiet the noise in my mind,
and help me rest in your presence
instead of my worries.

¡Amén!

"And be ye kind one to another, tenderhearted, forgiving one another, even as God for Christ's sake hath forgiven you."

(Ephesians 4:32, KJV)

Prayer for Understanding *Others*:

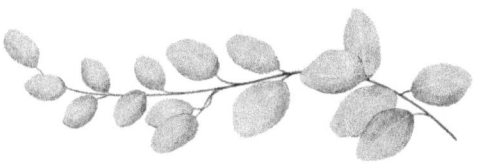

Diosito,

Help me understand those
whose experiences are not my own.
Open my *corazón*
to empathy and compassion.
Help me see the world
through their *ojitos,*
and treat everyone
with kindness and respect.

¡Amén!

"And let us not be weary in well doing: for in due season we shall reap, if we faint not."

(Galatians 6:9, KJV)

Prayer for

Perseverance:

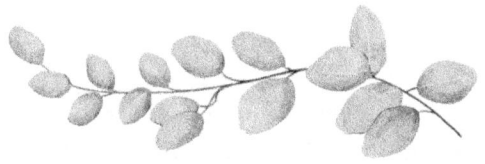

Diosito,

When I feel like saying,
"Ay, ya no puedo,"
give me the *fuerza* to *seguir adelante.*
Even when progress feels slow
and the road feels heavy,
help me trust that
every small step matters.
Keep my goals and dreams
close to my heart,
and help me move forward—
un paso a la vez.

¡Amén!

"Be strong and of a good courage, fear not, nor be afraid of them: for the Lord thy God, he it is that doth go with thee; he will not fail thee, nor forsake thee."

(Deuteronomy 31:6, KJV)

Prayer for
Courage:

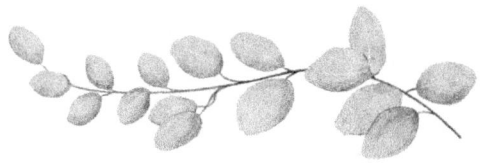

Diosito,

Give me the courage
to stop shrinking myself
just to feel comfortable.
When I start overthinking,
second-guessing myself,
or feeling too *apenada* to speak up,
remind me that my voice matters too.
And like my *mamá* says,
*"Si tu brillo les estorba,
que se pongan lentes."*
Help me trust the gifts
you placed in me
and walk confidently
into the spaces you are calling me to.

¡Amén!

"When thou hast eaten and art full, then thou shalt bless the Lord thy God for the good land which he hath given thee."

(Deuteronomy 8:10, KJV)

Prayer for
Before a Meal:

Diosito,

Thank you for this *comida*
that nourishes both body and soul.
Bless the hands that prepared it,
the earth that provided it,
and the *familia* at this table.
May we share not only food,
but also laughter, stories, and *amor*.
And *Diosito*,
please forgive me for the seconds
I'm definitely going to have.

¡Amén!

"And the King shall answer and say unto them, Verily I say unto you, Inasmuch as ye have done it unto one of the least of these my brethren, ye have done it unto me."

(Matthew 25:40, KJV)

Prayer for
Those in Need:

Diosito,

I pray for those who are suffering—
whether from illness, *sin lana,*
or feeling lonely.
Comfort them in their *dolor*
and provide them with the resources
they need.
Inspire me to be a source of *ayuda,*
to show up with kindness,
and to remember that
"donde come uno, comen dos."
Help me open my heart,
share what I can,
and never look away
when someone is hurting.

¡Amén!

"Now faith is the substance of things hoped for, the evidence of things not seen."

(Hebrews 11:1, KJV)

Prayer for
Stronger Faith:

Diosito,

Some days my faith feels strong...
and other days, it feels as shaky
as a folding chair at a *carne asada*.
Help me continue seeking you
in the quiet moments,
the hard moments,
and the everyday moments.
Strengthen my *corazón*,
remind me of your promises,
and help me trust that you are still
working—
even when life feels uncertain.
Keep my faith rooted in *amor*, *esperanza*,
and *gracia*.

¡Amén!

63

"But grow in grace, and in the knowledge of our Lord and Saviour Jesus Christ. To him be glory both now and for ever. Amen."

(2 Peter 3:18, KJV)

Prayer for
Spiritual Growth:

Diosito,

Guide me on my spiritual journey,
ayúdame.
Help me learn and grow
in my understanding of you.
Remind me that spiritual growth
doesn't happen overnight…
ni en un solo domingo.
Help me become
the kind of person
my *mamá* raised me to be.
Inspire me to live a *vida*
that makes you happy—
full of *amor* and *alegría.*

¡Amén!

"Commit thy works unto the Lord, and thy thoughts shall be established."

(Proverbs 16:3, KJV)

Prayer for Blessing Your
Business:

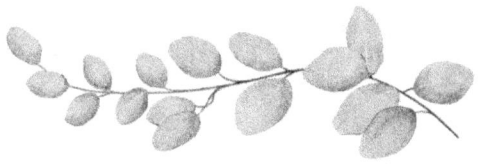

Diosito,

I dedicate this business to you,
con todo mi corazón.
Guide me and bless every *pasito* I take.
May it be a source of honest work—
providing for my *familia*
and contributing to others.
Give me wisdom in my decisions,
integrity in my actions,
and resilience through challenges.
May this business thrive,
not just for profit,
but as a reflection of your
amor y tu gracia.

¡Amén!

"Yea, though I walk through the valley of the shadow of death, I will fear no evil: for thou art with me; thy rod and thy staff they comfort me."

(Psalm 23:4, KJV)

Prayer for
Strength:

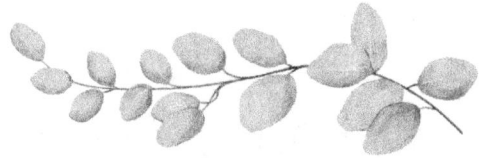

Diosito,

I ask for your *fortaleza*
to face whatever challenges
come my way today.
Give me the courage to persevere,
la sabiduría to make good *decisiones,*
and the *fe* to trust in your plan.
With you,
I am *fuerte* and *capaz.*

¡Amén!

"Now the God of hope fill you with all joy and peace in believing, that ye may abound in hope, through the power of the Holy Ghost."

(Romans 15:13, KJV)

Prayer for

Hope:

Diosito,

Even when things
se pongan bien feas,
remind me that there is always
esperanza—like when *abuela* finds
a forgotten *lotería* ticket.
Help me to see the light in the darkness,
to believe in *milagros,*
and to never give up on my *sueños.*

¡Amén!

"Be careful for nothing; but in every thing by prayer and supplication with thanksgiving let your requests be made known unto God. And the peace of God, which passeth all understanding, shall keep your hearts and minds through Christ Jesus."

(Philippians 4:6-7, KJV)

Prayer for
Anxiety:

Diosito,

My mind and body feel restless—
like I've had too much *cafecito...*
(aunque eso ni existe.)
Some days, the noise, the plans, and all the
expectations feel overwhelming.
There are moments when I want to cancel
everything, ignore my phone,
and disappear under my *cobijas.*
Slow my thoughts, *calma mi corazón,*
and help me breathe through
the *nervios* I carry.
Remind me that I don't have to
have it together all the time.
Wrap me in your *paz*
and help me feel grounded again.

¡Amén!

"Blessed are they that mourn: for they shall be comforted."

(Matthew 5:4, KJV)

Prayer for
Grief:

Diosito,

My heart feels heavy
with sorrow and loss.
Some days, the sadness comes quietly.
Other days, it hits all over again.
Stay close to me through the aching,
the remembering, and the moments
that feel empty without them.
Surround me with *amor*
and comfort me gently—
like *abuela's caldo* on the hardest days.
Remind me that love does not disappear,
and neither do the people
we carry in our *corazón.*

¡Amén!

"Endeavouring to keep the unity of the Spirit in the bond of peace."

(Ephesians 4:3, KJV)

Prayer for
Unity:

Diosito,

Help us come together
like a *familia* at a *quinceañera*—
united in love and respect.
Break down the *paredes*
that divide us,
and help us see the good
in each other.
May we work together
to create a more just
and peaceful *mundo*.

¡Amén!

"Defend the poor and fatherless:
do justice to the afflicted and
needy. Deliver the poor and
needy: rid them out of the hand
of the wicked."

(Psalm 82:3-4, KJV)

Prayer for the
Oppressed:

Diosito,

I lift up those
who are suffering
from injustice and oppression—
like those stuck in *la migra*.
Give them *fuerza,*
protect them from *daño,*
and inspire us
to fight for their *libertad.*
Help us create a world
where everyone is treated
with *dignidad y respecto.*

¡Amén!

"I will praise thee; for I am fearfully and wonderfully made: marvellous are thy works; and that my soul knoweth right well."

(Psalm 139:14, KJV)

Prayer for
Self-Love:

Diosito,

Help me see myself
through your *ojos*—as a beloved *hija,*
worthy of *amor y felicidad.*
Like when *abuela* says I'm her *favorita.*
Forgive my flaws, celebrate my strengths
and help me embrace
the person you created me to be.
May I treat myself
with kindness and compassion.

¡Amén!

"For if ye forgive men their trespasses, your heavenly Father will also forgive you: But if ye forgive not men their trespasses, neither will your Father forgive your trespasses."

(Matthew 6:14-15, KJV)

Prayer for

Forgiveness:

Diosito,

Help me forgive those who have hurt me,
just as you have forgiven me—
even when they took
the last *pan dulce.*
Release me from bitterness
and resentment,
and fill my heart with compassion.
May I learn from *el pasado*
and move forward with love.

¡Amén!

"Peace I leave with you, my peace I give unto you: not as the world giveth, give I unto you. Let not your heart be troubled, neither let it be afraid."

(John 14:27, KJV)

Prayer for
Inner Peace:

Diosito,

Grant me the serenity to accept the *cosas*
I cannot change, like when
a *novela* ends on a cliffhanger.
Give me the courage to change the things I
can, and the wisdom to know the difference.
Calm my *inquieto espíritu* and fill me
with your divine *paz*.

¡Amén!

"Wisdom is the principal thing;
therefore get wisdom: and with
all thy getting get
understanding."

(Proverbs 4:7, KJV)

Prayer for

Wisdom:

Diosito,

Guide my *pensamientos y acciones*
with your *sabiduría.*
Help me make choices
that align with your will
especially when life gets confusing
and my emotions get loud.
Lead me toward a
vida con propósito.
May I continue learning,
growing,
and *using my dones*
para servir a los demás.

¡Amén!

"Trust in the Lord with all thine heart; and lean not unto thine own understanding. In all thy ways acknowledge him, and he shall direct thy paths."

(Proverbs 3:5-6, KJV)

Prayer for
Trust:

Diosito,

Some days I want all the answers
right away—
with confirmations and *señales*.
Help me trust in your timing,
even when I don't understand
ni papa.
When my thoughts begin acting
bien dramáticas,
remind me that you are already
working things out behind the scenes.
Teach me to rest in your peace
instead of trying to control
every little thing.
Fill my *corazón* with *calma,*
esperanza, and trust in you.

¡Amén!

"And the second is like unto it, Thou shalt love thy neighbour as thyself."

(Matthew 22:39, KJV)

Prayer for
Neighbors:

Diosito,

Bless my *vecinos* and help us create a
comunidad of kindness *y apoyo.*
Open my *corazón* to see their *necesidades*
and inspire me to lend a helping hand.
May our *vecindario*
be a place of *paz* and *amistad.*

¡Amén!

"When my father and my mother forsake me, then the Lord will take me up."

(Psalm 27:10, KJV)

Prayer for Those Who Feel Alone:

Diosito,

Wrap your loving arms around those who
feel isolated and lonely.
Remind them that they are loved—
más que un Duvalín,
valued *más que oro,*
and never truly alone, *nunca.*
Guide me to reach out and offer un
cafecito y buena compañía
to those in need.

¡Amén!

"I will both lay me down in peace, and sleep: for thou, Lord, only makest me dwell in safety."

(Psalm 4:8, KJV)

Prayer for a
Restful Night:

Diosito,

As I lay my head down to rest,
fill my dreams with peace
and sweet *sueños de angelitos.*
Calm my worries, soothe my *alma,*
and if the *pesadillas* show up tonight,
hold me close through them too.
Prepare me for a new *día* filled with
oportunidades.
Thank you for your *protección*
and love.

¡Amén!

"Blessed are the peacemakers: for they shall be called the children of God."

(Matthew 5:9, KJV)

Prayer for Peace in the
World:

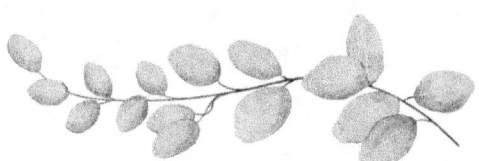

Diosito,

I pray for *paz* in our *mundo*,
especially in places torn by
tanto drama y violencia.
Soften *corazones duros,*
promote understanding,
and inspire leaders to seek
peaceful solutions.
May your love reign in every
esquina del mundo.

¡Amén!

"And the Lord God took the man, and put him into the garden of Eden to dress it and to keep it."

(Genesis 2:15, KJV)

Prayer for the Environment:

Diosito,

Bless our *planeta*—
nuestra madre tierra—
and help us be good *vecinos*
to your creation.
Guide us to make choices
that protect our environment for
future *generaciones.*
Inspire us to live in harmony
with nature and to appreciate
its *belleza* and abundance—
from the *montañas*—
under a quiet *estrella*—
to the *playas.*

¡Amén!

"For God hath not given us the spirit of fear; but of power, and of love, and of a sound mind."

(2 Timothy 1:7, KJV)

Prayer for Overcoming
Fear:

Diosito,

When *miedo* paralyzes me,
like the *cucuy* once did,
fill me with courage and strength.
Help me remember that you are always
conmigo—guiding me, protecting me
and walking beside me.
Give me the faith
to step outside my comfort zone
and pursue my dreams.

¡Amén!

"Train up a child in the way he should go: and when he is old, he will not depart from it."

(Proverbs 22:6, KJV)

Prayer for Our Children:

Diosito,

Bless our *niños y niñas*—
the light of our lives.
Guide their little feet on the right path,
from their first steps
to who they're becoming.
Protect them from all harm,
and fill their *corazones* with your love.
When the world gets loud,
let them still hear your voice
guiding them with light.
May they grow to be kind, compassionate,
and strong—
always remembering their roots—
the stories, the language, the love—
and the values we've taught them.

¡Amén!

"Have not I commanded thee? Be strong and of a good courage; be not afraid, neither be thou dismayed: for the Lord thy God is with thee whithersoever thou goest."

(Joshua 1:9, KJV)

Prayer for Moving to a
New Place:

Diosito,

As I embark on this new *aventura*
in a *nuevo lugar*
I ask for your guidance and *bendiciones.*
Help me adapt to my new surroundings,
make new *amigos,*
and find my place in this *comunidad.*
May my new *hogar* be filled with
amor, risas y paz.

¡Amén!

"And whatsoever ye do, do it heartily, as to the Lord, and not unto men; Knowing that of the Lord ye shall receive the reward of the inheritance: for ye serve the Lord Christ."

(Colossians 3:23-24, KJV)

Prayer for Starting a
New Job:

Diosito,

As I begin this new *chamba,* I ask for
your wisdom and *apoyo.*
Help me learn quickly, work well with
my colleagues, and make a positive
contribution to my workplace.
May my *trabajo* be fulfilling and
meaningful—like making *tamales* for the
familia—with love and purpose.

¡Amén!

"Commit thy works unto the
Lord, and thy thoughts shall be
established."

(Proverbs 16:3, KJV)

Prayer for Taking *Exams:*

Diosito,

As I prepare for my *exámenes,*
grant me *claridad* of mind,
focus, and recall.
Help me manage my *estrés*
and remember all that I have studied.
May I approach my exams
with *confianza* and do my best—
like I'm making
the perfect *arroz con leche.*

¡Amén!

"Honour thy father and mother;
which is the first commandment
with promise"

(Ephesians 6:2, KJV)

Prayer for
Parents:

Diosito,

I lift up my *padres* to you.
Gracias for blessing me with their *amor,*
guidance, and that endless *apoyo,*
even when I was a little *rebelde.*
Watch over them—*cuídalos*—
keep them healthy,
and *llena sus vidas* with *alegría y paz.*
Help me to always show them the respect
they deserve and cherish every moment
we have together.
May our bond grow stronger *cada día,*
rooted in love
and *fe.*

¡Amén!

"Wherefore, my beloved brethren, let every man be swift to hear, slow to speak, slow to wrath:"

(James 1:19, KJV)

Prayer for Patience with Technology:

Diosito,

When my phone freezes, my internet
crashes, and my computer is acting
bien dramática, dame paciencia.
Help me remember that technology
is a tool, not a test of my character
(aunque se siente así).
May I find solutions with a calm mind
and a sense of humor.
And if I still feel like throwing my
phone out the *ventana,*
remind me how much it cost...
porque no estoy para comprar otro.

¡Amén!

"Fear thou not; for I am with thee: be not dismayed; for I am thy God: I will strengthen thee; yea, I will help thee; yea, I will uphold thee with the right hand of my righteousness."

(Isaiah 41:10, KJV)

Prayer for Feeling *Lost*:

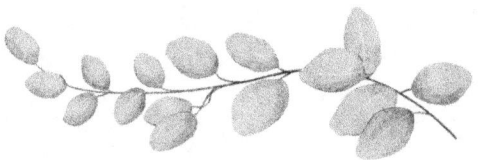

Diosita,

Lately, I've felt a little lost…
like I'm moving through life
without really knowing where I belong.
Some days, I feel stuck.
Other days, I feel like everyone else
has things figured out except me.
Ando perdida.
Remind me that I am not behind,
forgotten, or alone.
Help me reconnect with myself, with my
purpose, and with the person
you created me to be.
Even if I can only see one step at a time,
ayúdame a seguir adelante.

¡Amén!

"He shall cover thee with his feathers, and under his wings shalt thou trust: his truth shall be thy shield and buckler."

(Psalm 91:4, KJV)

Prayer for Protection Against Enemies:

Diosito,

Put a fence *de alambre* around me.
Protect my peace
from envy, *malas vibras,*
and people with bad intentions.
Don't let negativity
settle into my *corazón*
or distract me from my *propósito.*
Give me wisdom
to know who deserves access to me,
and strength to walk away
from what drains my spirit—
because sometimes
"mejor sola que mal acompañada."

¡Amén!

"A good name is rather to be chosen than great riches, and loving favour rather than silver and gold."

(Proverbs 22:1, KJV)

Prayer Against Tarnishing of

Name:

Diosito,

Protect my name
from *chismes, mentiras,*
and people who speak
without knowing my *corazón.*
Don't let *las chismosas*
stain my reputation
with stories that aren't true.
Help me move with integrity,
stay grounded in my *fe,*
and trust that the truth
will always come to light.
And when people misunderstand me,
remind me that
not every rumor
deserves my energy.

¡Amén!

"And we know that all things work together for good to them that love God, to them who are the called according to his purpose."

(Romans 8:28, KJV)

Prayer for
Motivation:

Diosito,

Ignite within me a fire of passion
and purpose.
When I feel lost or discouraged,
remind me of my potential
and the gifts you have given me.
Give me that *empujoncito*
to chase my *sueños*—
like a gentle *"ponte las pilas"*
when I need it most.
Help me make the world a better place.

¡Amén!

"Now no chastening for the present seemeth to be joyous, but grievous: nevertheless afterward it yieldeth the peaceable fruit of righteousness unto them which are exercised thereby."

(Hebrews 12:11, KJV)

Prayer for Discipline to Keep

Answered Prayers:

Diosito,

Thank you for the *bendiciones*
I once cried for.
Now give me the *disciplina*
to take care of them,
grow them,
and not take them for granted.
Help me stay focused, responsible,
and consistent—*siempre echándole ganas*—
even when the excitement fades
or life gets busy.
Teach me to protect
what once felt impossible.

¡Amén!

"Wherefore comfort yourselves
together, and edify one another,
even as also ye do."

(1 Thessalonians 5:11, KJV)

Prayer for
Work:

Diosito,

Bless my *trabajo* today.
Give me the *energía*
of a triple shot of *cafecito*
and the *motivación* to be my best.
Help me be productive, efficient,
and a *buena influencia*
on my *compañeros*.
May my work bring you honor—
and maybe
a little extra *feria* in my *bolsillo*.

¡Amén!

"Lo, children are an heritage of
the Lord: and the fruit of the
womb is his reward."

(Psalm 127:3, KJV)

Prayer for Children with Disabilities:

Diosito,

Thank you for the precious gift of children,
especially those with special needs.
They shine with a unique *luz* and teach us
about unconditional love and strength.
Bless them with your *gracia.*
Give them the support they need to thrive, and
fill their lives with joy and laughter.
Help us see their abilities,
not their disabilities,
and create a world where they are loved,
accepted, and celebrated.
May they always be surrounded
by people who see their magic
and remind them,
"Tu luz también merece brillar."

¡Amén!

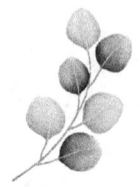

Note from the
author:

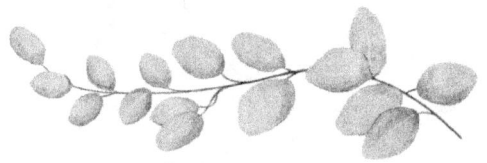

Diosito y Cafecito started as a way
for me to find peace and humor
in my own everyday struggles.
I pray it does the same for you.
Con mucho cariño.

Siempre recuerda,
Diosito está contigo.

"And even to your old age I am he;
and even to hoar hairs will I carry
you: I have made, and I will bear;
even I will carry, and will deliver
you."

(Isaiah 46:4, KJV)

More from
Evelyne Pérez:

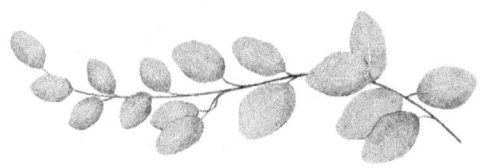

Children's Books
created with *corazón* and purpose:

Autism Series:
A New Friend
Un nuevo amigo
Trick Roar Treat
Buds vs Bullies

Brown y Brillante
Published by Know Culture

I'd love to hear your prayers,
your moments, and your
reflections.
Connect with me on Instagram
@evelynetheauthor

Con Diosito… todo.